squares
& slices

THE AUSTRALIAN
Women's Weekly

CONTENTS

AUSTRALIAN CUP AND SPOON MEASUREMENTS ARE METRIC. A CONVERSION CHART APPEARS ON PAGE 77.

Slices are the perfect cross between a biscuit and a cake, and the perfect time-saving treat. All the slices in this book are absolutely irresistible. My favourite are the best-ever fudge brownies on page 37. I make them all the time for my granddaughters and they love them.

Pamela Clark

Food Director

CARAMEL, HONEY AND CASHEW SLICE

prep + cook time 1 hour (+ refrigeration & cooling)
makes 30

2½ cups (375g) roasted salted cashews
⅓ cup (50g) plain (all-purpose) flour
¼ cup (55g) firmly packed light brown sugar
45g (1½ ounces) butter, melted
3 eggs
¼ cup (90g) honey
1 tablespoon honey, extra, warmed
pastry
1 cup (150g) plain (all-purpose) flour
¼ cup (40g) icing (confectioners') sugar
100g (3 ounces) cold butter, chopped coarsely
1 egg yolk
1 teaspoon iced water, approximately

1 Make pastry.
2 Grease 20cm x 30cm (8-inch x 12-inch) rectangular pan; line base and long sides with baking paper, extending paper 5cm (2 inches) over sides.
3 Roll pastry between sheets of baking paper until large enough to line base of pan. Lift pastry into pan; trim excess. Refrigerate 30 minutes.
4 Preheat oven to 180°C/350°F.
5 Bake pastry base 10 minutes, or until browned lightly; cool.
6 Reduce oven temperature to 160°C/325°F.
7 Combine nuts, flour, sugar, butter, eggs and honey in medium bowl. Pour mixture over base. Bake about 40 minutes; cool. Brush slice with extra honey before cutting.
pastry Process flour, icing sugar and butter until crumbly. Add egg yolk and enough of the water to make ingredients come together. Knead dough on floured surface until smooth.

tip Store slice in an airtight container for up to 3 days.

STICKY DATE SLICE

prep + cook time **40 minutes (+ cooling)** makes **12**

1⅓ cups (185g) coarsely chopped seeded
  dried dates
1⅓ cups (330ml) water
½ teaspoon bicarbonate of soda (baking soda)
60g (2 ounces) butter, softened
¾ cup (165g) firmly packed light brown sugar
2 eggs
1 cup (150g) self-raising flour
caramel topping
½ cup (110g) firmly packed light brown sugar
2 tablespoons water
20g (¾ ounce) butter
1 tablespoon golden syrup or treacle
1 cup (250ml) thickened (heavy) cream

1 Preheat oven to 180°C/350°F. Grease
24cm x 32cm (9½-inch x 13-inch) swiss roll
pan; line base and long sides with baking paper,
extending paper 5cm (2 inches) over sides.
2 Combine dates and the water in medium
saucepan; bring to the boil. Remove from heat;
stir in soda, stand 5 minutes.
3 Meanwhile, beat butter and sugar in medium
bowl with electric mixer until light and fluffy;
beat in eggs, one at a time. Stir in sifted flour,
then date mixture. Pour mixture into pan.
Bake about 20 minutes. Cool slice in pan.
4 Make caramel topping.
5 Cut slice into squares; top each square with
a dollop of caramel topping. Sprinkle with
chocolate curls, if you like.
caramel topping Stir sugar and the water
in small saucepan, over low heat, until sugar
dissolves. Bring to the boil; boil, uncovered,
4 minutes. Remove from heat; stir in butter
and syrup. Transfer mixture to small bowl; add
¼ cup (60ml) of the cream. Beat with electric
mixer until thickened slightly; cool. Beat
remaining cream in small bowl with electric
mixer until soft peaks form; beat in caramel
mixture until firm peaks form. Refrigerate
until required.

tip **Store slice in an airtight container in the fridge for up
to 3 days.**

BANOFFEE SLICE

prep + cook time **45 minutes (+ refrigeration)** makes **30**

1 cup (150g) self-raising flour
¼ cup (55g) caster (superfine) sugar
100g (3 ounces) butter, melted
2 medium bananas (400g), sliced
    thinly diagonally
1 cup (250ml) thickened (heavy) cream,
    whipped
60g (2 ounces) milk eating chocolate
caramel filling
395g (12½ ounces) canned sweetened
    condensed milk
90g (3 ounces) butter, chopped coarsely
½ cup (110g) firmly packed light brown sugar
2 tablespoons golden syrup or treacle

1 Preheat oven to 180°C/350°F. Grease 20cm x 30cm (8-inch x 12-inch) rectangular pan; line base and long sides with baking paper, extending paper 5cm (2 inches) over sides.
2 Combine sifted flour and sugar in small bowl; stir in butter. Press mixture firmly over base of pan. Bake about 20 minutes. Cool.
3 Meanwhile, make the caramel filling.
4 Pour filling over base. Refrigerate 1 hour or until firm.
5 Place banana over caramel; top with whipped cream. Grate chocolate, using a vegetable peeler; sprinkle over cream before cutting slice.
caramel filling Stir ingredients in medium saucepan over medium heat about 12 minutes or until caramel in colour. Cool 5 minutes.

tip **Slice is best eaten on the day it is made, however, it can be stored in an airtight container in the fridge for up to 2 days.**

HONEY NUT SQUARES

prep + cook time 50 minutes (+ cooling & refrigeration)
makes 35

125g (4 ounces) unsalted butter, softened
½ cup (110g) caster (superfine) sugar
1 egg yolk
1 cup (150g) plain (all-purpose) flour
⅓ cup (50g) self-raising flour
⅔ cup (240g) honey
⅓ cup (75g) firmly packed light brown sugar
90g (3 ounces) unsalted butter,
    chopped coarsely
2 tablespoons thickened (heavy) cream
1 cup (120g) pecans
½ cup (80g) almond kernels
½ cup (70g) roasted hazelnuts

1 Preheat oven to 160°C/325°F. Grease 20cm x 30cm (8-inch x 12-inch) rectangular pan; line base and long sides with baking paper, extending paper 5cm (2 inches) over sides.
2 Beat softened butter, caster sugar and egg yolk in small bowl with electric mixer until light and fluffy. Stir in sifted flours. Press mixture evenly over base of pan. Bake 15 minutes.
3 Stir honey, brown sugar and chopped butter in medium saucepan over low heat until sugar is dissolved. Bring to the boil; boil, uncovered, without stirring, 2 minutes. Add cream; boil, stirring, 1 minute. Remove from heat. Stir in nuts until coated in caramel mixture. Working quickly, pour nut mixture over base; spread evenly with spatula.
4 Bake about 15 minutes. Cool slice in pan. Refrigerate 2 hours before cutting.

tip Store squares in an airtight container for up to 4 days.

MILLIONAIRE'S SHORTBREAD

prep + cook time **50 minutes (+ cooling & refrigeration)**
makes **40**

125g (4 ounces) unsalted butter, softened
½ cup (110g) caster (superfine) sugar
1 egg yolk
1 cup (150g) plain (all-purpose) flour
⅓ cup (50g) self-raising flour
395g (12½ ounces) canned sweetened
condensed milk
30g (1 ounce) unsalted butter, extra
2 tablespoons golden syrup or treacle
1 cup (140g) roasted salted peanuts
200g (6½ ounces) milk eating chocolate,
chopped coarsely
2 teaspoons vegetable oil

1 Preheat oven to 160°C/325°F. Grease 20cm x 30cm (8-inch x 12-inch) rectangular pan; line base and long sides with baking paper, extending paper 5cm (2 inches) over sides.
2 Beat butter, sugar and egg yolk in small bowl with electric mixer until light and fluffy. Stir in sifted flours. Press mixture evenly over base of pan. Bake 15 minutes.
3 Meanwhile, stir condensed milk, extra butter and syrup in small saucepan, over medium heat, about 15 minutes or until mixture is golden brown. Working quickly, pour caramel over base; smooth surface with spatula. Press nuts into caramel with spatula. Bake 10 minutes; cool.
4 Stir chocolate and oil in small saucepan over low heat until smooth. Pour chocolate mixture over caramel. Refrigerate about 2 hours or until set before cutting.

tip **Store shortbread in an airtight container for up to 3 days.**

WHITE CHOCOLATE CARAMEL SLICE

prep + cook time **45 minutes** (+ cooling & refrigeration)
makes **20**

⅓ cup (30g) rolled oats
½ cup (75g) self-raising flour
2 teaspoons cocoa powder
⅓ cup (75g) firmly packed light brown sugar
½ cup (40g) desiccated coconut
90g (3 ounces) butter, melted
395g (12½ ounces) canned sweetened
    condensed milk
⅓ cup (115g) golden syrup or treacle
30g (1 ounce) butter, chopped coarsely
250g (6½ ounces) white eating chocolate,
    chopped coarsely
2 teaspoons vegetable oil

1 Preheat oven to 180°C/350°F. Grease 20cm x 30cm (8-inch x 12-inch) rectangular pan; line base and long sides with baking paper, extending paper 5cm (2 inches) over sides.
2 Process oats until finely chopped. Combine oats with sifted flour and cocoa in medium bowl. Stir in sugar, coconut and melted butter. Press mixture evenly over base of pan. Bake 10 minutes.
3 Combine condensed milk, syrup and chopped butter in small saucepan. Bring to the boil, stirring, about 5 minutes or until thickened. Pour mixture over base. Bake 10 minutes. Cool.
4 Stir chocolate and oil in small heatproof bowl over small saucepan of simmering water until smooth; spread over caramel. Refrigerate about 30 minutes or until set before cutting slice using a hot knife.

tip **Store slice in an airtight container in the fridge for up to 4 days.**

CARAMEL APPLE SLICE

prep + cook time **55 minutes (+ cooling & refrigeration)**
makes **24**

1 sheet butter puff pastry
125g (4 ounces) unsalted butter, softened
½ cup (110g) caster (superfine) sugar
2 eggs
¾ cup (90g) ground almonds
¼ cup (35g) plain (all-purpose) flour
1 teaspoon finely grated lemon rind
caramel apples
60g (2 ounces) unsalted butter
⅓ cup (75g) raw sugar
3 medium apples (450g), peeled, quartered,
cored, sliced thinly

1 Preheat oven to 180°C/350°F. Grease 20cm x 30cm (8-inch x 12-inch) rectangular pan; line base and long sides with baking paper, extending paper 5cm (2 inches) over sides.
2 Make caramel apples.
3 Roll pastry between sheets of baking paper until large enough to line base of pan. Press pastry into pan; trim edges. Refrigerate 20 minutes.
4 Beat butter and sugar in small bowl with electric mixer until light and fluffy; beat in eggs, one at a time. Stir in ground almonds, sifted flour and rind. Spread mixture over pastry in pan; top with caramel apples. Bake about 30 minutes. Cool slice in pan before cutting.
5 Reheat caramel sauce; drizzle over apples before serving.
caramel apples Melt the butter in large frying pan over medium heat; add the sugar and apple. Cook, stirring occasionally, about 5 minutes or until apple is lightly caramelised. Remove from heat; cool 20 minutes. Place apple in medium bowl; reserve caramel sauce in frying pan.

tip **Slice is best eaten on the day it is made.**

PEANUT, PLUM AND OAT SLICE

prep + cook time 45 minutes **makes** 32

1½ cups (225g) plain (all-purpose) flour
100g (3 ounces) butter, chopped coarsely
½ cup (110g) caster (superfine) sugar
¼ cup (60ml) cold water
1¼ cups (175g) coarsely chopped roasted
    unsalted peanuts
⅔ cup (60g) rolled oats
60g (2 ounces) butter, melted
½ cup (160g) plum jam

1 Preheat oven to 200°C/400°F. Grease
20cm x 30cm (8-inch x 12-inch) rectangular
pan; line base and long sides with baking paper,
extending paper 5cm (2 inches) over sides.
2 Process flour, chopped butter and
1 tablespoon of the sugar until crumbly.
Add the water; process until ingredients
come together. Press dough into pan; bake
15 minutes.
3 Meanwhile, combine peanuts, oats, melted
butter and remaining sugar in medium bowl.
4 Spread base with jam; sprinkle with peanut
mixture. Bake about 20 minutes. Cool slice in
pan before cutting.

tip Store slice in an airtight container for up to 3 days.

CHEWY CARROT AND WALNUT SLICE

prep + cook time **45 minutes** makes **24**

125g (4 ounces) butter, melted
1 cup (220g) firmly packed light brown sugar
1 egg
1½ cups (135g) rolled oats
¾ cup (75g) coarsely chopped walnuts
1 medium carrot (120g), grated finely
¾ cup (110g) plain (all-purpose) flour
¼ cup (35g) self-raising flour
lemon glaze
1 cup (160g) pure icing (confectioners') sugar
1 egg white
1 tablespoon lemon juice

1 Preheat oven to 180°C/350°F. Grease 20cm x 30cm (8-inch x 12-inch) rectangular pan; line base and long sides with baking paper, extending paper 5cm (2 inches) over sides.
2 Combine butter, sugar, egg, oats, nuts and carrot in medium bowl; stir in sifted flours. Spread mixture into pan; bake about 30 minutes.
3 Meanwhile, make lemon glaze.
4 Drizzle glaze over hot slice; bake about 5 minutes or until glaze forms a crust. Cool slice in pan before cutting.
lemon glaze Sift icing sugar into small bowl; stir in egg white and juice until smooth.

tip Store slice in an airtight container for up to 4 days.

CHERRY SQUARES WITH COCONUT ICE FROSTING

prep + cook time 35 minutes (+ refrigeration) makes 35

125g (4 ounces) butter, chopped coarsely
¼ cup (55g) caster (superfine) sugar
⅓ cup (60ml) light corn syrup
8 cups (320g) corn flakes
½ cup (40g) toasted shredded coconut
1 cup (100g) halved red glacé cherries
coconut ice frosting
1½ cups (240g) pure icing
   (confectioners') sugar
1 cup (80g) desiccated coconut
1 egg white
2 tablespoons boiling water, approximately
pink food colouring

1 Grease 20cm x 30cm (8-inch x 12-inch) rectangular pan; line base and long sides with baking paper, extending paper 5cm (2 inches) over sides.
2 Stir butter, sugar and syrup in small saucepan over low heat until sugar dissolves; bring to the boil. Reduce heat; simmer, uncovered, without stirring, 5 minutes.
3 Meanwhile, coarsely crush corn flakes with hands in large bowl until approximately half the volume; stir in coconut and cherries.
4 Stir butter mixture into cornflake mixture. Spread mixture into pan; press down firmly. Cover; refrigerate 30 minutes or until firm.
5 Make coconut ice frosting.
6 Spread frosting over slice; cut into squares when firm.

coconut ice frosting Sift icing sugar into medium bowl; stir in coconut and egg white until combined. Add enough of the water until icing is spreadable; tint frosting pale pink.

tip Store squares in an airtight container in the fridge for up to a week.

ANZAC SLICE WITH GOLDEN ICING

prep + cook time **1 hour (+ standing)** makes **40**

125g (4 ounces) unsalted butter,
    chopped coarsely
1 cup (220g) firmly packed light brown sugar
2 tablespoons golden syrup or treacle
¼ cup (60ml) water
½ teaspoon bicarbonate of soda
    (baking soda)
½ cup (40g) desiccated coconut
1 cup (90g) rolled oats
1 cup (150g) plain (all-purpose) flour
golden icing
2 cups (320g) icing (confectioners') sugar
1 tablespoon golden syrup or treacle
20g (¾ ounce) unsalted butter
2 tablespoons hot water, approximately

1 Preheat oven to 120°C/250°F. Grease 24cm x 32cm (9½-inch x 13-inch) swiss roll pan; line base and long sides with baking paper, extending paper 5cm (2 inches) over sides.
2 Stir butter, sugar and syrup in medium saucepan over low heat until sugar dissolves. Remove from heat. Stir in the combined water and soda. Stir in coconut, oats and sifted flour. Spread mixture into pan; bake about 45 minutes. Stand slice in pan 15 minutes before transferring to wire rack to cool.
3 Meanwhile, make golden icing.
4 Spread slice with icing; stand at room temperature until set before cutting.
golden icing Sift icing sugar into medium heatproof bowl; stir in syrup, butter and enough of the water to make a thick paste. Set bowl over medium saucepan of simmering water; stir until icing is spreadable.

tips **If you want the slice to be fudgy in texture decrease the baking time by 5 to 10 minutes. Store slice in an airtight container for up to a week.**

TROPICAL MUESLI SLICE

prep + cook time **55 minutes** makes **21**

125g (4 ounces) unsalted butter,
  chopped coarsely
⅓ cup (75g) firmly packed light brown sugar
2 tablespoons honey
1½ cups (135g) rolled oats
½ cup (75g) self-raising flour
1½ cups (225g) finely chopped dried
  tropical fruit
⅓ cup (25g) desiccated coconut

1 Preheat oven to 160°C/325°F. Grease 20cm x 30cm (8-inch x 12-inch) rectangular pan; line base and long sides with baking paper, extending paper 5cm (2 inches) over sides.
2 Stir butter, sugar and honey in medium saucepan over low heat until sugar dissolves. Stir in remaining ingredients. Press mixture firmly into pan. Bake about 40 minutes.
3 Cool slice in pan before cutting.

tips **We used dried pineapple, papaya and mango in this recipe. Store slice in an airtight container for up to a week.**

CHOCOLATE CRACKLE SLICE

prep + cook time **40 minutes (+ refrigeration)** makes **48**

185g (6 ounces) dark eating (semi-sweet)
   chocolate, chopped coarsely
100g (3 ounces) unsalted butter,
   chopped coarsely
½ cup (175g) golden syrup or treacle
4 cups (140g) rice bubbles
185g (6 ounces) dark eating (semi-sweet)
   chocolate, melted
2 teaspoons cocoa powder

1 Grease 20cm x 30cm (8-inch x 12-inch) rectangular pan; line base and long sides with baking paper, extending paper 5cm (2 inches) over sides.
2 Stir chopped chocolate and butter in medium saucepan over low heat until smooth. Remove from heat; stir in syrup and rice bubbles.
3 Spread melted chocolate over base of pan; top with rice bubble mixture, press down gently. Refrigerate 2 hours or until firm. Dust slice with sifted cocoa powder before cutting.

tip **Store slice in airtight container in fridge for up to a week.**

DRIED APPLE AND CRANBERRY MUESLI SLICE

prep + cook time **40 minutes** makes **24**

2 cups (220g) untoasted natural muesli
1 cup (150g) self-raising flour
½ cup (30g) coarsely chopped dried apples
½ cup (65g) dried cranberries
½ cup (110g) caster (superfine) sugar
155g (5 ounces) butter, chopped coarsely
¼ cup (90g) honey
2 eggs, beaten lightly
pink icing
½ cup (80g) icing (confectioners') sugar
1 tablespoon hot water
¼ teaspoon vegetable oil
pink food colouring

1 Preheat oven to 180°C/350°F. Grease 20cm x 30cm (8-inch x 12-inch) rectangular pan; line base and long sides with baking paper, extending paper 5cm (2 inches) over sides.
2 Combine muesli, sifted flour, fruit and sugar in large bowl.
3 Combine butter and honey in small saucepan; stir over low heat until smooth. Stir butter mixture and egg into muesli mixture until combined. Spread mixture into pan; bake about 25 minutes. Cool slice in pan.
4 Meanwhile, make pink icing. Drizzle icing over slice before cutting.
pink icing Combine sifted icing sugar, the water and oil in small bowl; tint icing pink.

tip **Store slice in an airtight container for up to a week.**

WICKED CHOC-MINT ROCKY ROAD

prep + cook time 15 minutes (+ refrigeration) **makes** 60

600g (1¼ pounds) dark eating (semi-sweet)
   chocolate, chopped coarsely
250g (8 ounces) white marshmallows
1 cup (140g) unsalted pistachios, roasted,
   chopped coarsely
½ cup (80g) blanched almonds, roasted,
   chopped coarsely
½ cup (40g) shredded coconut, toasted
2 cups (375g) mint leaf lollies

1 Grease 20cm x 30cm (8-inch x 12-inch)
rectangular pan; line base and long sides with
baking paper, extending paper 5cm (2 inches)
over sides.
2 Stir chocolate in large heatproof bowl over
large saucepan of simmering water until smooth.
Working quickly, stir in remaining ingredients;
spread mixture into pan. Refrigerate 3 hours or
overnight before cutting into pieces.

tips To roast nuts and toast coconut, spread evenly
onto an oven tray then cook in a moderate oven for
about 5 minutes. Alternatively, stir over low heat in a
heavy-based frying pan, watching closely to avoid
burning. The mint leaves used in this recipe are
sometimes called spearmint leaves – they are a firm
leaf-shaped, mint-flavoured confection. Store rocky
road in an airtight container in the fridge for up to
2 weeks. Slice is best served at room temperature.

WHITE CHOCOLATE, PINEAPPLE AND COCONUT SLICE

prep + cook time **55 minutes (+ standing)** makes **35**

90g (3 ounces) butter, chopped coarsely
250g (8 ounces) white eating chocolate,
chopped coarsely
440g (14 ounces) canned crushed pineapple
in natural juice
½ cup (110g) caster (superfine) sugar
2 eggs
1½ cups (225g) plain (all-purpose) flour
½ cup (75g) self-raising flour
½ cup (40g) desiccated coconut
1½ cups (240g) pure icing
(confectioners') sugar
⅓ cup (25g) shredded coconut

1 Preheat oven to 160°C/325°F. Grease 24cm x 32cm (9½-inch x 13-inch) swiss roll pan; line base and long sides with baking paper, extending paper 5cm (2 inches) over sides.
2 Stir butter and chocolate in medium saucepan over low heat until smooth. Cool 10 minutes.
3 Meanwhile, drain pineapple well over medium bowl. Reserve 2 tablespoons juice.
4 Stir caster sugar, eggs, sifted flours, desiccated coconut and drained pineapple into chocolate mixture; spread mixture into pan. Bake about 35 minutes. Cool slice in pan before icing.
5 Meanwhile, sift icing sugar into medium heatproof bowl; stir in reserved pineapple juice. Set bowl over medium saucepan of simmering water; stir until icing is spreadable.
6 Spread icing over slice; sprinkle with shredded coconut. Stand at room temperature until icing sets before cutting.

tips **Do not overheat or over-stir chocolate mixture or it will "split". Store slice in an airtight container for up to a week.**

BEST-EVER FUDGE BROWNIES

prep + cook time **1 hour** makes **96**

185g (6 ounces) unsalted butter,
    chopped coarsely
300g (10½ ounces) dark eating (semi-sweet)
    chocolate, chopped coarsely
¼ cup (25g) cocoa powder
1 cup (220g) firmly packed light brown sugar
¾ cup (165g) caster (superfine) sugar
2 teaspoons vanilla extract
4 eggs
1½ cups (225g) plain (all-purpose) flour
2 teaspoons cocoa powder, extra

1 Preheat oven to 170°C/340°F. Grease
20cm x 30cm (8-inch x 12-inch) rectangular
pan; line base and long sides with baking paper,
extending paper 5cm (2 inches) over sides.
2 Stir butter and chocolate in medium
saucepan over low heat until smooth. Remove
from heat; whisk in sifted cocoa, sugars and
extract until smooth.
3 Stir eggs and sifted flour into chocolate
mixture. Pour mixture into pan; spread evenly.
4 Bake about 40 minutes. Cool brownie in pan.
Dust with extra sifted cocoa before cutting.

tips The mixture should be barely warm when the eggs
and flour are added. Use a bamboo skewer to test if
the brownie is cooked. The skewer should feel moist if
you want a fudgy brownie; if not, bake the brownie
another 5 minutes or so. Store in an airtight container in
the fridge for up to a week. They are best served at
room temperature.

CAPPUCCINO MOUSSE SQUARES

prep + cook time **25 minutes (+ refrigeration)** makes **24**

250g (8 ounces) plain chocolate biscuits
155g (5 ounces) unsalted butter, melted
1 cup (250ml) thickened (heavy)
   cream, whipped
2 teaspoons cocoa powder
cappuccino mousse filling
185g (6 ounces) dark eating (semi-sweet)
   chocolate, melted
1 egg, separated
2 teaspoons instant coffee granules
⅓ cup (80ml) thickened (heavy)
   cream, whipped
¼ cup (55g) caster (superfine) sugar

1 Grease 20cm x 30cm (8-inch x 12-inch) rectangular pan; line base and long sides with baking paper, extending paper 5cm (2 inches) over sides.
2 Process biscuits until fine. Add butter; process until combined. Press mixture over base of pan. Refrigerate 30 minutes.
3 Meanwhile, make cuppuccino mousse filling.
4 Spread filling over biscuit base in pan. Cover; refrigerate 3 hours or overnight until set.
5 Spread whipped cream over mousse filling; dust with sifted cocoa powder.
cappuccino mousse filling Combine melted chocolate, egg yolk and coffee in medium bowl; fold in cream. Beat egg white and sugar in small bowl with electric mixer until thick and sugar dissolves. Fold into chocolate mixture, in two batches.

tips **Use un-iced, unfilled plain biscuits for this recipe. Store squares in an airtight container in the fridge for up to 4 days.**

COFFEE PECAN SLICE

prep + cook time **1 hour (+ cooling)** makes **24**

125g (4 ounces) butter, softened
¼ cup (55g) caster (superfine) sugar
1 cup (150g) plain (all-purpose) flour
¼ cup (35g) self-raising flour
2 cups (280g) pecans, roasted
coffee topping
2 teaspoons instant coffee granules
3 teaspoons boiling water
2 eggs
½ cup (175g) golden syrup or treacle
⅓ cup (75g) firmly packed light brown sugar
60g (2 ounces) butter, melted
2 tablespoons plain (all-purpose) flour

1 Preheat oven to 200°C/400°F. Grease 20cm x 30cm (8-inch x 12-inch) rectangular pan; line base and long sides with baking paper, extending paper 5cm (2 inches) over sides.
2 Beat butter and sugar in small bowl with electric mixer until light and fluffy. Stir in sifted flours, in two batches. Press dough over base of pan. Bake 10 minutes. Cool 10 minutes. Reduce oven temperature to 180°C/350°F.
3 Meanwhile, make the coffee topping.
4 Pour topping over base; top with single layer of nuts. Bake about 25 minutes or until set. Cool slice in pan before cutting.

coffee topping Dissolve coffee in the boiling water in medium heatproof bowl. Whisk in eggs, syrup, sugar, butter and flour until combined.

tips To roast nuts, spread evenly onto an oven tray then cook in a moderate oven for about 5 minutes. Alternatively, stir over low heat in a heavy-based frying pan, watching closely to avoid burning. Store slice in an airtight container for up to a week.

PEANUT BUTTER AND JAM BROWNIES

prep + cook time **55 minutes** makes **24**

155g (5 ounces) unsalted butter,
  chopped coarsely
360g (11½ ounces) dark eating (semi-sweet)
  chocolate, chopped coarsely
1½ cups (330g) firmly packed light
  brown sugar
3 eggs
¾ cup (110g) plain (all-purpose) flour
½ cup (120g) sour cream
½ cup (120g) raspberry jam, warmed, strained
peanut butter filling
⅓ cup (95g) smooth peanut butter
45g (1½ ounces) unsalted butter, melted
¼ cup (40g) icing (confectioners') sugar

1 Preheat oven to 160°C/325°F. Grease
24cm x 32cm (9½-inch x 13-inch) swiss roll
pan; line base and long sides with baking paper,
extending paper 5cm (2 inches) over sides.
2 Make peanut butter filling.
3 Stir butter and chocolate in medium
saucepan over low heat until smooth. Remove
from heat; stir in sugar, then eggs, sifted flour
and sour cream. Spread mixture into pan.
4 Drop alternate rounded teaspoons of peanut
butter filling and jam onto brownie mixture; swirl
together using a skewer.
5 Bake about 40 minutes. Cool brownie in pan
before cutting.
peanut butter filling Combine all ingredients
in small bowl.

tip **Store brownies in airtight container for up to a week.**

CHOC-RASPBERRY LAMINGTON SLICE

prep + cook time **45 minutes** (+ refrigeration) makes **30**

6 eggs
⅔ cup (150g) caster (superfine) sugar
⅓ cup (50g) cornflour (cornstarch)
½ cup (75g) plain (all-purpose) flour
⅓ cup (50g) self-raising flour
1 cup (250ml) thickened (heavy) cream
½ cup (160g) raspberry jam
1 cup (80g) desiccated coconut
chocolate icing
4½ cups (720g) icing (confectioners') sugar
½ cup (50g) cocoa powder
15g (½ ounce) butter, melted
½ cup (125ml) milk, approximately

1 Preheat oven to 180°C/350°F. Grease two 24cm x 32cm (9½-inch x 13-inch) swiss roll pans; line bases and long sides with baking paper, extending paper 5cm (2 inches) over sides.
2 To make sponges, beat eggs in medium bowl with electric mixer about 10 minutes or until thick and creamy; gradually add sugar, beating until dissolved. Fold in triple-sifted flours.
3 Divide and spread sponge mixture between pans. Bake about 15 minutes. Turn cakes immediately onto baking-paper-covered wire racks to cool.
4 Beat cream in small bowl with electric mixer until firm peaks form.
5 Spread one cake with jam, then with cream to within 1cm (½ inch) of the edge of the sponge. Top with remaining cake; place on wire rack.
6 Make chocolate icing; spread icing all over top and sides of slice. Sprinkle top and sides with coconut; refrigerate until set before cutting.
chocolate icing Sift icing sugar and cocoa into medium heatproof bowl; stir in butter and enough milk to make a thick paste. Set bowl over medium saucepan of simmering water; stir until icing is spreadable.

tips **Leaving a 1cm (½-inch) border of sponge without cream will make the icing of the sides of the slice easier to do. The weight of the top layer of sponge will push the cream far enough. Store slice in an airtight container in the fridge for up to 3 days.**

CARAMEL CHEESECAKE SLICE

prep + cook time 1 hour (+ refrigeration & cooling)
makes 48

200g (6½ ounces) plain sweet biscuits
½ cup (60g) pecans, roasted
100g (3 ounces) unsalted butter, melted
380g (12 ounces) canned caramel top'n'fill
cheesecake filling
500g (1 pound) cream cheese, softened
2 teaspoons vanilla extract
½ cup (110g) caster (superfine) sugar
2 eggs
1 cup (250ml) thickened (heavy) cream

1 Grease 20cm x 30cm (8-inch x 12-inch)
rectangular pan; line base and long sides with
baking paper, extending paper 5cm (2 inches)
over sides.
2 Process biscuits and nuts until fine. Add
butter; process until combined. Press mixture
evenly over base of pan. Refrigerate 30 minutes.
3 Preheat oven to 140°C/280°F.
4 Make cheesecake filling.
5 Spread caramel over biscuit base; pour
cheesecake filling over caramel. Bake about
45 minutes. Cool cheesecake in oven with
door ajar. Refrigerate 3 hours or overnight
before cutting.
cheesecake filling Beat cream cheese, extract,
sugar and eggs in medium bowl with electric
mixer until smooth. Gradually beat in cream.

tips We used digestive biscuits in this recipe. To roast
nuts, spread evenly onto an oven tray then cook in a
moderate oven for about 5 minutes. Alternatively, stir
over low heat in a heavy-based frying pan, watching
closely to avoid burning. Store slice in an airtight container
in the fridge for up to 2 days.

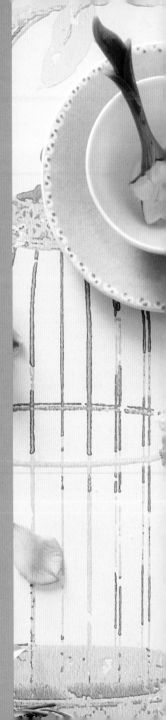

GINGER LIME SLICE

prep + cook time 40 minutes (+ refrigeration) makes 32

¾ cup (110g) plain (all-purpose) flour
¼ cup (55g) self-raising flour
½ teaspoon bicarbonate of soda (baking soda)
1 teaspoon each ground ginger and
   mixed spice
¼ cup (55g) firmly packed light brown sugar
65g (2 ounces) butter, chopped coarsely
½ cup (175g) golden syrup or treacle
1 egg, beaten lightly
½ cup (125ml) milk
lime filling
1 teaspoon gelatine
2 tablespoons lime juice
250g (8 ounces) cream cheese, softened
¼ cup (55g) caster (superfine) sugar
2 teaspoons finely grated lime rind
1 cup (250ml) pouring cream

1 Preheat oven to 180°C/350°F. Grease two 24cm x 32cm (9½-inch x 13-inch) swiss roll pans; line bases and long sides with baking paper, extending paper 5cm (2 inches) over sides.
2 To make ginger cake, sift flours, soda and spices into large bowl; stir in brown sugar. Combine butter and syrup in small saucepan; stir over low heat until smooth. Stir butter mixture into flour mixture with egg and milk. Divide mixture between pans; bake about 10 minutes. Cool in pans.
3 Meanwhile, make lime filling.
4 Pour filling over one of the ginger cakes in pan; top with remaining ginger cake. Refrigerate 3 hours or overnight until firm before cutting.
lime filling Sprinkle gelatine over juice in small heatproof jug; stand jug in small saucepan of simmering water. Stir until gelatine dissolves. Cool 5 minutes. Beat cream cheese, sugar and rind in medium bowl with electric mixer until smooth; beat in cream. Stir in gelatine mixture.

tip **Store slice in an airtight container in the fridge for up to a week.**

STRAWBERRY CUSTARD SLICE

prep + cook time **40 minutes (+ cooling & refrigeration)**
makes **15**

⅔ cup (160ml) milk
½ cup (125ml) pouring cream
1 vanilla bean
4 egg yolks
¼ cup (55g) caster (superfine) sugar
2 tablespoons cornflour (cornstarch)
1¼ cups (185g) plain (all-purpose) flour
¼ cup (40g) icing (confectioners') sugar
125g (4 ounces) unsalted butter,
   chopped coarsely
2 teaspoons iced water, approximately
250g (8 ounces) strawberries, sliced thinly
2 tablespoons raspberry jam,
   warmed, strained

1 Grease 20cm x 30cm (8-inch x 12-inch) rectangular pan; line base and long sides with baking paper, extending paper 5cm (2 inches) over sides.

2 Combine milk and cream in medium saucepan. Split vanilla bean; scrape seeds into cream mixture, add bean. Bring cream mixture to the boil. Whisk 3 of the egg yolks, caster sugar and cornflour in small bowl until combined. Discard vanilla bean from cream mixture; gradually whisk hot cream mixture into egg mixture. Return to pan; cook, whisking, until custard mixture boils and thickens. Cool.

3 Meanwhile, blend or process flour, icing sugar and butter until crumbly. Add remaining egg yolk and enough of the water to make ingredients cling together. Knead dough on floured surface until smooth. Press dough over base of pan; prick all over with a fork. Cover with plastic wrap; refrigerate 30 minutes.

4 Preheat oven to 200°C/400°F.

5 Bake base about 15 minutes or until browned lightly; cool.

6 Spread custard over base; top with berries. Brush slice with jam; refrigerate 1 hour before cutting.

tip **Slice is best eaten within 24 hours.**

WHITE CHOCOLATE AND RASPBERRY SWIRL CHEESECAKE

prep + cook time **30 minutes (+ refrigeration)** makes **16**

250g (8 ounces) plain sweet biscuits
155g (5 ounces) butter, melted
3 teaspoons gelatine
2 tablespoons boiling water
375g (12 ounces) cream cheese, softened
2 tablespoons caster (superfine) sugar
1 cup (250ml) thickened (heavy) cream
1 teaspoon vanilla extract
200g (6½ ounces) white eating chocolate,
 melted, cooled
raspberry topping
1½ cups (225g) frozen raspberries, thawed
1 tablespoon icing (confectioners') sugar
1 teaspoon gelatine
1 tablespoon boiling water

1 Grease 20cm x 30cm (8-inch x 12-inch) rectangular pan; line base and long sides with baking paper, extending paper 5cm (2 inches) over sides.
2 Process biscuits until fine. Add butter; process until combined. Press mixture over base of pan. Refrigerate 30 minutes.
3 Sprinkle gelatine over the water in small heatproof jug; stand jug in small saucepan of simmering water. Stir until gelatine dissolves. Cool 5 minutes.
4 Make raspberry topping.
5 Beat cream cheese and sugar in medium bowl with electric mixer until smooth. Beat in cream, extract and chocolate until combined. Stir in gelatine mixture. Pour over biscuit base.
6 Spoon raspberry topping over cream cheese mixture; swirl with a skewer. Refrigerate 3 hours or overnight before cutting.

raspberry topping Process raspberries until smooth; strain puree into small bowl, discard seeds. Stir sifted icing sugar into puree. Sprinkle gelatine over the water in small heatproof jug; stand jug in small saucepan of simmering water. Stir until gelatine dissolves. Cool 5 minutes. Stir mixture through raspberry puree.

tip **Store slice in an airtight container in the fridge for up to 4 days.**

CHOCOLATE HONEYCOMB ICE-CREAM SLICE

prep + cook time **1 hour (+ freezing & standing)**
makes **15**

1.5 litres (6 cups) vanilla ice-cream,
    softened slightly
½ cup (65g) finely chopped unsalted
    pistachios, roasted
150g (4½ ounces) chocolate-coated
    honeycomb bars, chopped finely
125g (4 ounces) unsalted butter, softened
⅓ cup (55g) caster (superfine) sugar
⅓ cup (55g) firmly packed light brown sugar
½ teaspoon vanilla extract
1 egg
¾ cup (110g) plain (all-purpose) flour
¾ cup (110g) self-raising flour
¼ cup (25g) cocoa powder

1 Line 20cm x 30cm (8-inch x 12-inch) rectangular pan with four layers of plastic wrap, extending plastic wrap 10cm (4 inches) over sides of pan.

2 Place ice-cream in large bowl; fold in nuts and chocolate-coated honeycomb. Working quickly, spoon ice-cream into pan, pressing down firmly and smoothing surface. Fold plastic wrap over to enclose. Freeze 3 hours or overnight until firm.

3 Preheat oven to 170°C/340°F. Remove ice-cream from pan, still wrapped in plastic; place on tray. Return to freezer.

4 Grease two 20cm x 30cm (8-inch x 12-inch) rectangular pans; line bases and long sides with baking paper, extending paper 5cm (2 inches) over sides.

5 To make cookie dough, beat butter, sugars and extract in small bowl with electric mixer until light and fluffy; beat in egg. Transfer mixture to large bowl; stir in sifted flours and cocoa.

6 Divide dough in half; press into pans. Bake about 10 minutes. Stand cookie slices in pans 20 minutes before turning, top-side up, onto wire racks to cool.

7 Place one cookie slice on board; top with ice-cream then remaining cookie slice. Cut into squares; serve immediately.

tips **To roast nuts, spread evenly onto an oven tray then cook in a moderate oven for about 5 minutes. Alternatively, stir over low heat in a heavy-based frying pan, watching closely to avoid burning. If you are not serving the slice immediately, return to the freezer until required. Stand at room temperature for about 5 minutes before cutting.**

LEMON CHEESECAKE SQUARES

prep + cook time **20 minutes (+ refrigeration)** makes **24**

250g (8 ounces) butternut snap biscuits
½ cup (40g) flaked almonds
125g (4 ounces) butter, melted
250g (8 ounces) cream cheese, softened
3 teaspoons finely grated lemon rind
395g (12½ ounces) canned sweetened
  condensed milk
⅓ cup (80ml) lemon juice

1 Grease 20cm x 30cm (8-inch x 12-inch) rectangular pan; line base and long sides with baking paper, extending paper 5cm (2 inches) over sides.
2 Process biscuits and nuts until fine. Add butter; process until combined. Press mixture over base of pan. Refrigerate 30 minutes.
3 Beat cream cheese and rind in medium bowl with electric mixer until smooth. Add condensed milk and juice; beat until smooth. Pour cream cheese mixture over base. Refrigerate overnight before cutting.

tip **Store squares in an airtight container in the fridge for up to 4 days.**

HONEY AND SPICE SLICE

prep + cook time **1 hour (+ refrigeration & cooling)**
makes **20**

250g (8 ounces) gingernut biscuits
100g (3 ounces) butter, melted
500g (1 pound) cream cheese, softened
¼ cup (55g) caster (superfine) sugar
¼ cup (90g) honey
1 teaspoon vanilla extract
2 teaspoons mixed spice
½ cup (125ml) pouring cream
2 eggs, separated
2 teaspoons cinnamon sugar

1 Grease 20cm x 30cm (8-inch x 12-inch) rectangular pan; line base and long sides with baking paper, extending paper 5cm (2 inches) over sides.
2 Process biscuits until fine. Add butter; process until combined. Press mixture over base of pan; refrigerate 30 minutes.
3 Preheat oven to 160°C/325°F.
4 Beat cream cheese, sugar, honey, extract and spice in medium bowl with electric mixer until smooth; beat in cream and egg yolks.
5 Beat egg whites in small bowl with electric mixer until soft peaks form; fold into cream cheese mixture.
6 Pour cream cheese mixture over base; bake about 30 minutes. Cool in oven with door ajar. Refrigerate 3 hours or overnight. Sprinkle with cinnamon sugar before cutting.

tip **Store slice in an airtight container in the fridge for up to 4 days.**

RASPBERRY WALNUT SLICE

prep + cook time 55 minutes (+ cooling) **makes** 20

150g (4½ ounces) butter, softened
⅔ cup (110g) icing (confectioners') sugar
1¾ cups (260g) plain (all-purpose) flour
½ teaspoon ground cinnamon
½ cup (60g) ground walnuts
300g (9½ ounces) frozen raspberries

1 Preheat oven to 180°C/350°F. Grease
20cm x 30cm (8-inch x 12-inch) rectangular
pan; line base and long sides with baking paper,
extending paper 5cm (2 inches) over sides.
2 Beat butter and sifted icing sugar in medium
bowl with electric mixer until light and fluffy.
Stir in sifted flour, cinnamon and nuts until
mixture is crumbly.
3 Reserve 1 cup of crumble mixture. Press
remaining mixture into pan; top with
raspberries. Sprinkle with reserved crumble
mixture; bake about 40 minutes. Cool slice in
pan before cutting.

tips Walnut halves or pieces can be ground finely in a
blender or processor. Store slice in an airtight container
for up to 3 days.

FRUIT & NUT

APPLE CINNAMON CUSTARD-SQUARES

prep + cook time **50 minutes** makes **15**

100g (3 ounces) butter, softened
¼ cup (55g) caster (superfine) sugar
1 egg
⅔ cup (100g) self-raising flour
2 tablespoons custard powder
2 large apples (400g), quartered, cored,
    sliced thinly
20g (¾ ounce) butter, melted
2 teaspoons caster (superfine) sugar, extra
½ teaspoon ground cinnamon
custard
1 tablespoon custard powder
2 tablespoons caster (superfine) sugar
½ cup (125ml) milk
10g (⅓ ounces) butter
1 teaspoon vanilla extract

1 Make custard.
2 Preheat oven to 180°C/350°F. Grease
20cm x 30cm (8-inch x 12-inch) rectangular
pan; line base and long sides with baking paper,
extending paper 5cm (2 inches) over sides.
3 Beat softened butter and sugar in small
bowl with electric mixer until light and fluffy.
Beat in egg until combined. Stir in sifted flour
and custard powder.
4 Spread mixture into pan; top with custard.
Arrange apple on custard; brush with melted
butter. Sprinkle with combined extra sugar
and cinnamon.
5 Bake about 35 minutes; cool slice in pan before
cutting. Serve warm or at room temperature.
custard Combine custard powder and sugar
in small saucepan; gradually blend in milk.
Stir over heat until mixture boils and thickens
slightly. Remove from heat; stir in butter and
extract. Press plastic wrap over surface of
custard to prevent a skin forming; cool. Whisk
until smooth just before using.

tips **We used unpeeled red-skinned apples for this
recipe. Store squares in an airtight container in the
fridge for up to 3 days.**

FRUIT MINCE SQUARES

prep + cook time **30 minutes** makes **20**

155g (5 ounces) butter, softened
⅔ cup (150g) caster (superfine) sugar
2 eggs
1 cup (150g) self-raising flour
½ cup (75g) plain (all-purpose) flour
½ cup (125ml) milk
¾ cup (250g) fruit mince
¼ cup (20g) flaked almonds
2 teaspoons icing (confectioners') sugar

1 Preheat oven to 180°C/350°F. Grease 24cm x 32cm (9½-inch x 13-inch) swiss roll pan; line base and long sides with baking paper, extending paper 5cm (2 inches) over sides.
2 Beat butter and sugar in small bowl with electric mixer until light and fluffy. Beat in eggs, one at a time. Stir in sifted flours and milk. Spread mixture into pan; drop tablespoons of fruit mince over dough. Using the back of a spoon, swirl fruit mince through cake mixture; sprinkle with nuts.
3 Bake about 20 minutes. Dust with sifted icing sugar before cutting. Serve warm or at room temperature.

tips **We used fruit mince bought in a jar from the supermarket, but home-made would be even better. Store squares in an airtight container for up to 3 days.**

GARIBALDI SLICE

prep + cook time **50 minutes (+ refrigeration & cooling)**
makes **24**

1½ cups (240g) currants
½ cup (80g) sultanas
½ cup (75g) raisins
½ cup (125ml) water
2 tablespoons dry sherry
1 egg, beaten lightly
2 tablespoons caster (superfine) sugar
pastry
2 cups (300g) plain (all-purpose) flour
⅓ cup (75g) caster (superfine) sugar
185g (6 ounces) cold butter,
    chopped coarsely
2 egg yolks
1 tablespoon iced water, approximately

1 Preheat oven to 180°C/350°F. Grease
24cm x 32cm (9½-inch x 13-inch) swiss roll pan.
2 Make pastry.
3 Combine fruit, the water and sherry in small
saucepan; stir over low heat about 5 minutes
or until liquid is absorbed and fruit soft.
Blend or process fruit mixture until mixture is
smooth. Cool.
4 Roll one portion of pastry between sheets of
baking paper until large enough to line base of
pan; lift pastry into pan, trimming to fit. Spread
fruit mixture over pastry. Roll remaining pastry
until large enough to cover fruit; lift pastry over
fruit mixture, trimming to fit. Press down firmly.
Cut top layer of pastry into 24 rectangles; prick
each rectangle all over with a fork. Brush pastry
with egg; sprinkle with sugar.
5 Bake about 30 minutes. Cool slice in pan
before cutting.
pastry Sift flour and sugar into medium bowl;
rub in butter. Stir in egg yolks and enough of
the water to make a firm dough. Knead dough
on floured surface until smooth. Divide dough
in half; cover, refrigerate 30 minutes.

tip **Store slice in an airtight container for up to 3 days.**

CRANBERRY AND NUT NOUGAT SLICE

prep + cook time **30 minutes (+ refrigeration)** makes **48**

4 sheets confectioners' rice paper
2 tablespoons milk
20g (¾ ounce) butter
375g (12 ounces) white chocolate Melts
410g (13 ounces) pink and white
**   marshmallows, chopped coarsely**
1 cup (130g) dried cranberries
½ cup (70g) unsalted shelled
**   pistachios, roasted**
½ cup (80g) blanched almonds, roasted

1 Grease 24cm x 32cm (9½-inch x 13-inch) swiss roll pan; line base with 2 sheets of rice paper, trimming to fit.
2 Combine milk, butter and Melts in medium heatproof bowl over medium saucepan of simmering water; stir until smooth. Add marshmallows; stir until smooth. Remove from heat; stir in cranberries and nuts.
3 Spread mixture into pan; smooth surface. Top with remaining rice paper, trimming to fit. Place a second swiss roll pan on top of slice. Weight with cans; refrigerate overnight.
4 Turn slice onto board before cutting.

tips Rice paper is edible and ready to use. It can be bought from specialty food stores; don't confuse this paper with the rice paper used in recipes such as rice paper rolls, which needs soaking to soften. To roast nuts, spread evenly onto an oven tray then cook in a moderate oven for about 5 minutes. Alternatively, stir over low heat in a heavy-based frying pan, watching closely to avoid burning. Store slice in an airtight container in the fridge for up to a week.

CHOCOLATE AND ORANGE POLENTA SQUARES

prep + cook time 45 minutes (+ cooling & refrigeration)
makes 20

180g (6 ounces) dark eating (semi-sweet)
 chocolate, melted
½ cup (120g) sour cream
½ cup (110g) caster (superfine) sugar
90g (3 ounces) unsalted butter, softened
1 cup (150g) self-raising flour
½ cup (85g) polenta
⅓ cup (40g) ground almonds
2 teaspoons finely grated lemon rind
orange glaze
½ cup (80g) pure icing (confectioners') sugar
½ teaspoon finely grated orange rind
1 tablespoon orange juice

1 Preheat oven to 180°C/350°F. Grease
20cm x 30cm (8-inch x 12-inch) rectangular
pan; line base and long sides with baking
paper then a strip of foil, extending paper
5cm (2 inches) over sides.
2 Spread chocolate evenly over foil in base of
pan. Refrigerate about 10 minutes or until set.
3 Meanwhile, beat sour cream, sugar and
butter in small bowl with electric mixer until
smooth and creamy. Add sifted flour and
remaining ingredients. Beat on medium speed
about 3 minutes or until mixture is changed to
a paler colour; spread over chocolate.
4 Bake about 25 minutes. Cool slice in pan
10 minutes, then refrigerate about 30 minutes
or until chocolate sets.
5 Make orange glaze.
6 Turn slice top-side down onto board,
carefully remove paper and foil from base.
Turn slice top-side up; spread slice with glaze.
Refrigerate until set before cutting.
orange glaze Combine ingredients in small bowl.

tip Store squares in an airtight container in the fridge for
up to 3 days.

CHEWY PISTACHIO AND ALMOND SLICE

prep + cook time **50 minutes (+ cooling)** makes **30**

1 cup (160g) blanched almonds, roasted
1 cup (140g) unsalted shelled
    pistachios, roasted
1½ cups (240g) icing (confectioners') sugar
1 egg
2 egg whites
green food colouring
1⅓ cups (110g) flaked almonds

1 Preheat oven to 170°C/340°F. Grease 20cm x 30cm (8-inch x 12-inch) rectangular pan; line base and long sides with baking paper, extending paper 5cm (2 inches) over sides.
2 Process blanched almonds and pistachios until fine. Combine nuts and sifted icing sugar in medium bowl; stir in egg and egg whites. Tint mixture green with colouring.
3 Sprinkle half the flaked almonds over base of pan. Drop spoonfuls of mixture over nuts; carefully spread mixture over nuts with a spatula. Sprinkle slice with remaining flaked almonds; press down firmly.
4 Bake about 30 minutes. Cool slice in pan before cutting.

tips Store slice in an airtight container for up to a week. To roast nuts, spread evenly onto an oven tray then cook in a moderate oven for about 5 minutes. Alternatively, stir over low heat in a heavy-based frying pan, watching closely to avoid burning.

ALMONDS flat, pointy-tipped nuts with a pitted brown shell enclosing a creamy white kernel which is covered by a brown skin.
blanched brown skins removed.
flaked paper-thin slices.
meal also called ground almonds.
slivered small pieces cut lengthways.

BAKING PAPER also known as parchment paper or baking parchment – is a silicone-coated paper that is primarily used for lining baking pans and oven trays so cakes and biscuits won't stick, making removal easy.

BAKING POWDER a raising agent consisting mainly of two parts cream of tartar to one part bicarbonate of soda.

BICARBONATE OF SODA (BAKING SODA) an acid and alkaline combination, which when moistened and heated, gives off carbon dioxide that aerates and lightens the mixture during baking.

BISCUITS also known as cookies.
butternut snap crunchy cookie made with golden syrup, oats and coconut.
gingernuts a plain biscuit made with golden syrup and ginger.
shortbread plain buttery biscuit with a crumbly texture.

BUTTER we use salted butter unless stated otherwise; 125g is equal to 1 stick (4 ounces).

CASHEWS plump, kidney-shaped, golden-brown nuts with a distinctive sweet, buttery flavour and containing about 48 per cent fat. Because of this high fat content, they should be kept, sealed tightly, under refrigeration to avoid becoming rancid.

CHOCOLATE
choc bits also known as chocolate chips or chocolate morsels; available in milk, white and dark chocolate. They hold their shape in baking and are ideal for decorating.
dark eating also known as semi-sweet or luxury chocolate; made of a high percentage of cocoa liquor and cocoa butter, and little added sugar. Unless stated otherwise, we use dark eating chocolate in this book as it's ideal for use in desserts and cakes.
Melts small discs of compound milk, white or dark chocolate ideal for melting and moulding.
milk most popular eating chocolate, mild and very sweet; similar in make-up to dark with the difference being the addition of milk solids.
white contains no cocoa solids but derives its sweet flavour from cocoa butter. Very sensitive to heat.

CINNAMON available both in the piece (called sticks or quills) and ground into powder; one of the world's most common spices, used universally as a sweet, fragrant flavouring for both sweet and savoury foods.

CINNAMON SUGAR a combination of ground cinnamon and caster sugar. It is available from supermarkets in the spice section.

COCO POPS chocolate-flavoured puffed rice breakfast cereal.

COCOA POWDER also known as unsweetened cocoa; cocoa beans (cacao seeds) that have been fermented, roasted, shelled, ground into powder then cleared of most of the fat content.

COCONUT
desiccated concentrated, dried, unsweetened, finely shredded coconut.
shredded unsweetened thin strips of dried coconut flesh.

CONFECTIONERS' RICE PAPER is made from a dough made from the pith of an Asian shrub called the rice-paper plant (or rice-paper tree), not from rice. It resembles a grainy sheet of paper and is used in confectionery and baking. It can be bought from specialty food stores; don't confuse it with the rice paper used in recipes such as Asian rice paper rolls, which needs soaking to soften.

CORN FLAKES breakfast cereal made of dehydrated then baked crisp flakes of corn.

CORN SYRUP, LIGHT an imported product available in some supermarkets, delicatessens and health food stores. Made from cornstarch, it is a popular ingredient in American cooking for frostings, jams and jellies.

CORNFLOUR also known as cornstarch. Available made from corn or wheat (wheaten cornflour gives a lighter texture in cakes); used as a thickening agent in cooking.

CRANBERRIES fruit available dried and frozen; have a rich, astringent flavour and can be used in cooking sweet and savoury dishes. The dried version can usually be substituted for or with other dried fruit.

CREAM we used fresh cream, also known as pure or pouring cream unless otherwise stated. It contains no additives and has a minimum fat content of 35 per cent.

sour a thick commercially cultured soured cream with a minimum fat content of 35 per cent.

thick (double) a dolloping cream with a minimum fat content of 45 per cent.

thickened (heavy) a whipping cream containing thickener. Minimum fat content of 35 per cent.

CREAM CHEESE commonly called philadelphia or philly; a soft cow's milk cheese, its fat content ranges from 14 to 33 per cent.

CREME FRAICHE a mature, naturally fermented cream (minimum fat content 35 per cent) with a velvety texture and slightly tangy, nutty flavour. This French variation of sour cream can boil without curdling and be used in sweet and savoury dishes.

CURRANTS, DRIED tiny, almost black raisins so-named after a grape that originated in Corinth, Greece.

CUSTARD POWDER instant powdered mixture used to make pouring custard; similar to North American instant pudding mixes.

EGGS we use large chicken eggs weighing an average of 60g unless stated otherwise in the recipes in this book. If a recipe calls for raw or barely cooked eggs, exercise caution if there is a salmonella problem in your area, particularly in food eaten by children and pregnant women.

EXTRACT/ESSENCE an essence is either a distilled concentration of a food quality or an artificial creation of it. An extract is made by extracting the flavour from a food product. Essences and extracts keep indefinitely if stored in a cool dark place.

FLOUR

plain also known as all-purpose; unbleached wheat flour is the best for baking: the gluten content ensures a strong dough and a light result.

potato is made from cooked potatoes that have been dried and ground into a fine flour.

rice a very fine flour, made from ground rice.

self-raising all-purpose plain or wholemeal flour with baking powder and salt added; make yourself with plain or wholemeal flour sifted with baking powder in the proportion of 1 cup flour to 2 teaspoons baking powder.

FRUIT MINCE also known as mincemeat. A mixture of dried fruits such as raisins, sultanas and candied peel, nuts, spices, apple, brandy or rum. Is used as a filling for cakes, puddings and fruit mince pies.

GELATINE we use dried (powdered) gelatine in this book; it's also available in sheet form known as leaf gelatine. A thickening agent made from either collagen, a protein found in animal connective tissue and bones, or certain algae (agar-agar). Three teaspoons of dried gelatine (8g or one sachet) is about the same as four gelatine leaves. The two types are interchangable but leaf gelatine gives a much clearer mixture than dried gelatine; it's perfect in dishes where appearance matters.

GLACE CHERRIES or candied cherries; boiled in heavy sugar syrup then dried.

GLACE GINGER fresh ginger root preserved in sugar syrup.

GLUCOSE SYRUP also known as liquid glucose, made from wheat starch; used in jam and confectionery and available at health food stores and supermarkets.

GOLDEN SYRUP a by-product of refined sugarcane; pure maple syrup or honey can be substituted. Treacle is more viscous, and has a stronger flavour and aroma than golden syrup (which has been refined further and contains fewer impurities, so is lighter in colour and more fluid).

GROUND GINGER also called powdered ginger; used as a flavouring in baking but cannot be substituted for fresh ginger.

HAZELNUTS also known as filberts; plump, grape-sized, rich, sweet nut having a brown skin that is removed by rubbing heated nuts together vigorously in a tea-towel. Hazelnut meal is made by grounding the hazelnuts to a coarse flour texture for use in baking or as a thickening agent.

HONEY the variety sold in a squeezable container is not suitable for the recipes in this book.

JAM also known as preserve or conserve; most often made from fruit.

LOLLIES a confectionery also known as sweets or candy.

MACADAMIAS native to Australia; fairly large, slightly soft, buttery rich nut. Used to make oil and macadamia butter; equally good in salads or cakes and pastries; delicious eaten on their own. Should always be stored in the fridge to prevent their high oil content turning them rancid.

MARMALADE a preserve, usually based on citrus fruit.

MARSALA a fortified Italian wine produced in the region surrounding the Sicilian city of Marsala.

MARSHMALLOWS pink and white; made from sugar, glucose, gelatine and cornflour.

MILK we use full-cream homogenised milk unless otherwise specified.

evaporated unsweetened canned milk from which water has been extracted by evaporation. Evaporated skim or low-fat milk has 0.3 per cent fat content.

full-cream powder instant powdered milk made from whole cow milk with liquid removed and emulsifiers added.

sweetened condensed a canned milk product consisting of milk with more than half the water content removed and sugar added to the remaining milk.

MIXED DRIED FRUIT a combination of sultanas, raisins, currants, mixed peel and cherries.

MIXED SPICE a classic spice mixture generally containing caraway, allspice, coriander, cumin, nutmeg and ginger, although cinnamon and other spices can be added. It is used with fruit and in cakes.

MUESLI also known as granola, a combination of grains (mainly oats), nuts and dried fruits. Some manufacturers toast their product in oil and honey, adding crispness and kilojoules.

NOUGAT a popular confection in southern Europe; made from sugar or honey, roasted nuts, sometimes candied fruits and beaten egg white (for soft nougat) or caramelised sugar (for hard nougat).

NUTMEG a strong, pungent spice ground from the dried nut of an evergreen tree native to Indonesia. Usually found ground but the flavour is more intense from a whole nut, available from spice shops, so it's best to grate your own.

PEANUTS also known as groundnut, not in fact a nut but the pod of a legume. We mainly use raw (unroasted) or unsalted roasted peanuts.

PEANUT BUTTER peanuts ground to a paste; available in crunchy and smooth varieties.

PECANS native to the US and now grown locally; pecans are golden brown, buttery and rich. Walnuts are a good substitute.

PISTACHIOS green, delicately flavoured nuts inside hard off-white shells. Available salted or unsalted in their shells; you can also buy shelled.

POLENTA also known as cornmeal; a flour-like cereal made of dried corn (maize). Also the dish made from it.

RAISINS dried sweet grapes (traditionally muscatel grapes).

RHUBARB a plant with long, green-red stalks; becomes edible when cooked.

RICE BUBBLES a small puffed rice breakfast cereal.

ROLLED OATS flattened oat grain rolled into flakes and traditionally used for porridge. Instant oats are also available, but we prefer to use traditional oats for baking.

SHERRY fortified wine consumed as an aperitif or used in cooking. Sold as fino (light, dry), amontillado (medium sweet, dark) and oloroso (full-bodied, very dark).

STAR ANISE a dried star-shaped pod with seeds with an astringent aniseed flavour; commonly used to flavour stocks and marinades.

SUGAR we use coarse, granulated table sugar, also known as crystal sugar, unless otherwise specified.

brown a soft, finely granulated sugar retaining molasses for its characteristic colour and flavour.

caster also known as superfine or finely granulated table sugar.

demerara small-grained golden-coloured crystal sugar.

icing also known as confectioners' sugar or powdered sugar; pulverised granulated sugar crushed together with a small amount of cornflour.

pure icing also called confectioners' sugar or powdered sugar.

raw natural brown granulated sugar.

SULTANAS dried sweet grapes of the sultana variety.

VANILLA BEAN dried, long, thin pod from a tropical golden orchid; the minuscule black seeds inside the bean are used to impart a luscious vanilla flavour in baking and desserts. Place a whole bean in a jar of sugar to make the vanilla sugar often called for in recipes; a bean can be used three or four times.

extract obtained from vanilla beans infused in water; a non-alcoholic version of essence.

WALNUTS as well as being a good source of fibre and healthy oils, nuts contain a range of vitamins, minerals and other beneficial plant components called phytochemicals. Walnuts contain the beneficial omega-3 fatty acids.

WEET-BIX also known as ruskets; wholewheat malted breakfast biscuit.

CONVERSION CHART

MEASURES

One Australian metric measuring cup holds approximately 250ml, one Australian metric tablespoon holds 20ml, one Australian metric teaspoon holds 5ml.

The difference between one country's measuring cups and another's is within a 2- or 3-teaspoon variance, and will not affect your cooking results. North America, New Zealand and the United Kingdom use a 15ml tablespoon. All cup and spoon measurements are level. The most accurate way of measuring dry ingredients is to weigh them. When measuring liquids, use a clear glass or plastic jug with metric markings.

We use large eggs with an average weight of 60g.

DRY MEASURES

METRIC	IMPERIAL
15g	½oz
30g	1oz
60g	2oz
90g	3oz
125g	4oz (¼lb)
155g	5oz
185g	6oz
220g	7oz
250g	8oz (½lb)
280g	9oz
315g	10oz
345g	11oz
375g	12oz (¾lb)
410g	13oz
440g	14oz
470g	15oz
500g	16oz (1lb)
750g	24oz (1½lb)
1kg	32oz (2lb)

LIQUID MEASURES

METRIC	IMPERIAL
30ml	1 fluid oz
60ml	2 fluid oz
100ml	3 fluid oz
125ml	4 fluid oz
150ml	5 fluid oz
190ml	6 fluid oz
250ml	8 fluid oz
300ml	10 fluid oz
500ml	16 fluid oz
600ml	20 fluid oz
1000ml (1 litre)	1¾ pints

LENGTH MEASURES

METRIC	IMPERIAL
3mm	⅛in
6mm	¼in
1cm	½in
2cm	¾in
2.5cm	1in
5cm	2in
6cm	2½in
8cm	3in
10cm	4in
13cm	5in
15cm	6in
18cm	7in
20cm	8in
23cm	9in
25cm	10in
28cm	11in
30cm	12in (1ft)

OVEN TEMPERATURES

These oven temperatures are only a guide for conventional ovens. For fan-forced ovens, check the manufacturer's manual.

	°C (CELSIUS)	°F (FAHRENHEIT)
Very slow	120	250
Slow	150	275-300
Moderately slow	160	325
Moderate	180	350-375
Moderately hot	200	400
Hot	220	425-450
Very hot	240	475

The imperial measurements used in these recipes are approximate only. Measurements for cake pans are approximate only.

INDEX

Published in 2012 by ACP Books, Sydney

ACP Books are published by ACP Magazines Limited,
a division of Nine Entertainment Co.

54 Park St, Sydney
GPO Box 4088, Sydney, NSW 2001.

phone (+61)2 9282 8618; fax (+61)2 9126 3702

acpbooks@acpmagazines.com.au; www.acpbooks.com.au

ACP BOOKS

General Manager · Christine Whiston

Editor-in-Chief · Susan Tomnay

Creative Director · Hieu Chi Nguyen

Food Director · Pamela Clark

Published and Distributed in the United Kingdom by Octopus Publishing Group

Endeavour House

189 Shaftesbury Avenue

London WC2H 8JY

United Kingdom

phone (+44)(0)207 632 5400; fax (+44)(0)207 632 5405

info@octopus-publishing.co.uk;

www.octopusbooks.co.uk

Printed by Toppan Printing Co., China

International Foreign Language Rights - Brian Cearnes, ACP Books bcearnes@acpmagazines.com.au

A catalogue record for this book is available from the British Library.

ISBN 978-1-74245-237-1

© ACP Magazines Ltd 2012

ABN 18 053 273 546